PICTURING SCOTLAND

DUMFRIES & GALLOWAY

NESS PUBLISHING

2   Lovely Loch Ken lies in the heart of Dumfries & Galloway, a narrow ribbon of a loch stretching over 10 miles north to south from New Galloway to Townhead of Greenlaw.

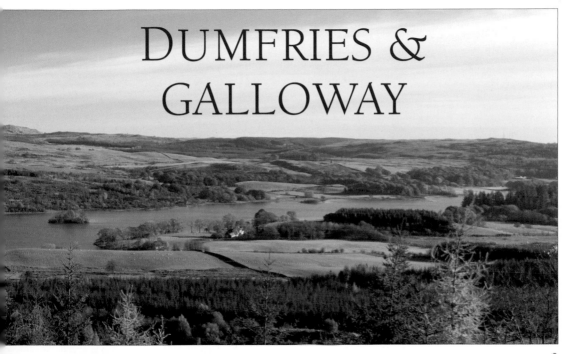

DUMFRIES & GALLOWAY

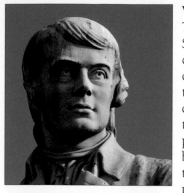

Welcome to Dumfries & Galloway!

This is the land that occupies the south-western corner of Scotland, a region of great scenic variety, historical riches and cultural activity. Dramatic ancient stone settings provide windows onto mankind's early influence; many castles and abbeys testify to aspects of life in medieval times; and today various towns celebrate local (and not so local) culture in a host of festivals throughout the year. A pivotal moment in Scottish history took place in Dumfries. Robert the Bruce and John Comyn were bitter rivals for the Scottish throne. On the 10th February 1306 the two men met in the Franciscan Priory, with Bruce intent on persuading Comyn that his claim to the throne was the better one. Persuasion apparently failed. Bruce attacked and slew Comyn, thus, for good or ill, setting Scotland on a course that has shaped its destiny ever since. This event is commemorated in the mural pictured opposite. Robert Burns, Scotland's Bard, spent the last years of his life in Dumfries up to his death in 1796.

Dumfries & Galloway was created in 1975 out of the traditional counties of Dumfriesshire in the east and Wigtownshire in the west, with the Stewartry of Kirkcudbright filling the middle territory, the land that lies between the rivers Nith and Cree. The name of Galloway harkens back to an ancient Gaelic kingdom born in the Dark Ages which managed to retain a degree of autonomy from the Scottish monarchy until the 13th century. Although created as a Scottish

FRIARS VENNEL ONCE THE SITE OF
GREYFRIARS MONASTRY WHERE IN 1306
ROBERT THE BRUCE
SLEW THE RED COMYN AIDED BY SIR ROGER
KIRKPATRICK AND OPENED THE FINAL STAGE FOR
SCOTTISH INDEPENDENCE WHICH ENDED
VICTORIOUSLY AT BANNOCKBURN 1314
'I MAK SICCAR'

This large mural in Friars' Vennel, Dumfries, illustrates the death of John Comyn at the hands of   5
Robert the Bruce in the priory that once stood here (see text opposite).

Region, Dumfries & Galloway became a Unitary Authority in 1996, the third largest in the country with an area of 2,480 square miles, equating to about 8% of Scotland's land area. The journey from the Mull of Galloway (the southernmost tip of Scotland) to where Dumfriesshire meets neighbouring Scottish Borders is one of around 110 miles. However, it is only 12th largest in terms of population due to its largely rural nature, being home to approximately 148,000 people.

Dumfries & Galloway also borders England, a factor which has been instrumental in the rise to fame of the villages of Gretna and Gretna Green. In the 18th century a tightening up of marriage regulations in England meant it was then easier to wed in Scotland, leading to couples eloping over the border from England to take advantage of this. Over time, the idea of marrying in Gretna Green became the zenith of romantic aspiration for courting couples, such that today an astonishing 4,000 weddings a year take place in the two villages. The Old Blacksmith's Shop in Gretna Green has become the epicentre of this 'industry'.

6 This giant pair of joined hands is outside The Old Blacksmith's Shop in Gretna Green (see text above)

Despite their administrative unification, Dumfriesshire and Galloway are diverse in character. Wigtownshire and Kirkcudbrightshire (as the Stewartry was latterly known) also have different claims to fame. Whithorn, in Wigtownshire, is the cradle of Christianity in Scotland because of its association with Scotland's first saint, Ninian. Wigtown itself is Scotland's National Book Town and home of the annual Wigtown Book Festival. From around 1850 the town of Kirkcudbright became an artists' colony. It began with the emergence of the Faed family of acclaimed artists from Gatehouse of Fleet and ended with the death, in 1949, of Jessie M. King who, with her husband E.A. Taylor, settled in Kirkcudbright from 1920. During this time, E.A. Hornel also became established there as an artist of note.

Now the scene is set, we embark on our tour, beginning in Dumfries then circuiting its county, before heading west through Kirkcudbright and on into Wigtownshire. A feast of visual treats awaits. . .

Greengate House, the home of Jessie M. King and her husband E.A. Taylor, leading lights of the artists' colony in Kirkcudbright

8 Dumfries is well described by its soubriquet of 'Queen of the South'. This elegant town sits astride the River Nith at its lowest bridging point. There has been a stone bridge on this site since 1432.

The structure seen here dates from 1620 as flooding had washed away its predecessor. It is named Devorgilla Bridge after Devorgilla, the mother of King John Balliol.

10 The busy and stylish centre of Dumfries. With a population of approximately 31,600 it is the largest town in the region. It was founded as a Royal Burgh in 1168.

Left: the 1707-built Midsteeple served as the town's tolbooth and prison. Right: Greyfriars Church 11 dates from 1868. The statue in the foreground is of Robert Burns. Inset: floral display by Greyfriars.

12 Around 1800 the Nith was narrowed by raising the level of the land on its east bank (right of picture) as a flood defence measure. On the far side of the river is the Robert Burns Centre.

Left: Just to the left of the picture opposite stands this suspension bridge, erected in 1875. **13**
Top right: bridge detail. Lower right: Hole I' the Wa' Inn was probably frequented by Robert Burns.

14 Robert Burns and his family lived in this cottage in Dumfries from May 1793. Left: the parlour. Right: Burns' bedroom. The cottage is open to the public.

Left: statue of Jean Armour, Burns' wife, in Dumfries. She gave birth to their ninth child on the day of Burns' funeral. Right: Burns' Mausoleum stands in St Michael's churchyard, Dumfries.

16 This former windmill is part of Dumfries Museum and houses a Camera Obscura on the top floor. This intriguing device gives fascinating panoramic views over the town.

Left: a heron on the Nith in Dumfries. It was being harried by seagulls at the time. **17**
Right: early spring in Castledykes Park, Dumfries. The castle was destroyed in 1357.

18 On the south side of Dumfries lies the Crichton University and College campus which includes 100 acres of landscaped gardens, of which the rock garden pictured here is a part.

The imposing late-Victorian Crichton Memorial Church is also part of the campus and is a popular venue for graduations and weddings.

20 Now we leave Dumfries and head for Gretna Green on the border with England. The Famous Blacksmith's Shop is the ancient building that made Gretna Green famous and has stood since 1712.

For reasons explained in the introduction (see p.6), it became one of the earliest destinations for **21** runaway couples. This is the original Marriage Room, presented as it was in the 1700s.

22 Nine miles west of Gretna is the attractive town of Annan, third largest in Dumfries & Galloway, with its many red stone buildings. This is the High Street.

Continuing westwards we come to the village of Ruthwell. The church houses this magnificent early **23** 8th-century Anglian carved cross. It is the most important Anglo-Saxon cross in Scotland.

24 A brief diversion now to take in this lovely winter scene in upper Annandale, north Dumfriesshire. The hills around here rise to as much as 800m/2624ft.

26 Returning south to our main route, the next point of interest is the superb, moated Caerlaverock Castle, the epitome of a medieval stronghold. Its triangular construction is unusual.

North of Caerlaverock on the road to Dumfries, from the village of Glencaple this glorious sunset **27** scene looks across the Nith estuary to Criffel in eastern Galloway.

28 Moving back inland and eastwards to the village of Ecclefechan, this is the birthplace of Thomas Carlyle (1795-1881), the great Scottish essayist, author and historian. Open to the public in summer.

North-west now to Lochmaben, a pleasing little town surrounded by three lochs. This view taken **29** from near the War Memorial is to the south, with Castle Loch just visible.

30 Four miles east of Lochmaben is Lockerbie. As the picture shows, it sits amid an undulating rural landscape which it serves. Dryfesdale Parish Church is prominent towards the left.

A longer hop east brings us to Langholm, known locally as the 'Muckle Toon'. Situated at the confluence of three rivers, the scene pictured is where Ewes Water joins the River Esk.

32 Left: travelling north from Langholm up Esk Dale reveals the most unexpected sight in Dumfriesshire, the Kagyu Samye Ling Tibetan Buddhist Centre. Right: Grey Mare's Tail waterfall near Moffat.

Climbing up past the Grey Mare's Tail (fifth highest waterfall in the UK) brings the more **33** adventurous walker to Loch Skeen, seen here with vivid ice patterns decorating its surface.

34 Following the Moffat Water from the Grey Mare's Tail leads to the market and (former) spa town of Moffat itself. Left: this statue reflects the quality of Moffat wool. Right: War Memorial.

Moffat can claim to be Scotland's first spa town following the discovery of a mineral spring in 1633, **35** followed by another in 1748. This view across the town looks towards Swatte Fell.

36 North-west of Moffat and nestling in the Lowther Hills is the lead-mining village of Wanlockhead, also the highest in Scotland at 468m/1531ft. A visit to the Lead Mining Museum is a 'must',

not least because it involves going inside one of the mines. There are also reconstructions of miners' **37** cottages in different centuries, the one seen here representing around 1910.

38 Leaving Wanlockhead in a south-westerly direction entails traversing the dramatic Mennock Pass, through which the road makes a twisting descent between the steep-sided hills.

Above: Sanquhar is also home to the oldest working Post Office in the world, established in 1712.

Left: turn right at Mennock and it's a short distance to Sanquhar. Its Tolbooth was erected in 1735 to the design of William Adam. Intact to this day, its Palladian façade graces the High Street.

40 South-east of Sanquhar in a tributary valley of Nithsdale is this vista which showcases Dumfriesshire scenery at its best. The village of Durisdeer sits in the centre of the scene with the Lowther Hills

providing a splendid backdrop – the Southern Upland Way passes over these tops. The region's agriculture is demonstrated by the mixture of arable and livestock farming.

42 Just a couple of miles south of Durisdeer is the magnificent Drumlanrig Castle. Constructed from distinctive pink sandstone, it was commissioned in 1691 by William Douglas, the first Duke of

Queensberry, and represents one of the first and most important Renaissance buildings in the country. Pictured above is the sumptuously furnished Drawing Room.

44 Continuing southwards, this is Ellisland Farm, leased by Robert Burns from 1788-1791. Three of his children were born here. Today visitors can explore and enjoy this important part of Burns' life.

And so to Galloway; first stop is New Abbey, south of Dumfries. This is Shambellie House, home of **45** the National Museum of Costume. The displays span the styles and fashions of the last two centuries.

46 New Abbey is a charming and historic village located just north of Criffel (see p.27). Amongst its many beauty spots is the millpond, built to serve the corn mill via the sluice gate on the right.

In full working order, the water-powered New Abbey Corn Mill has been carefully restored and is **47** operated regularly in summer months to demonstrate to visitors how oatmeal is produced.

48 Viewed from the north on a slightly misty morning, we see New Abbey itself. However, it has commonly been known as Sweetheart Abbey for centuries. It was founded in 1273 by Lady Devorgilla

in memory of her husband John Balliol. She carried his embalmed heart with her until her own death; in recognition of this devotion, the monks began to refer to the Abbey as Sweetheart Abbey.

50 Galloway is rightly famed for its wonderful coastline. A particularly notable stretch is the Colvend Coast from Sandyhills to Kippford. Rockcliffe, seen here, lies within this area.

It's a pleasant walk from Rockcliffe to Kippford, where, remarkably, the beach is composed not of **51** sand, or of shingle, but shells. Inset: close-up of the shell beach.

52 Left: Orchardton Tower is unique amongst Scotland's castles in being the only circular one!
Right: the town of Castle Douglas boasts several fine buildings, including its library.

Castle Douglas is situated inland north of the Colvend Coast. Carlingwark Loch, at the southern **53** end of the town, is a local beauty spot appreciated by residents and visitors alike.

54 Just west of Castle Douglas, on an island in the River Dee stands Threave Castle, a massive 14th-century tower built by Archibald the Grim, Lord of Galloway, around 1369.

The Threave Estate is also nearby, which comprises four main elements: the restored Scottish **55** baronial-style Threave House (above), Threave Garden, Sculpture Garden and Nature Reserve.

56 Screel Hill (343m/1125ft) rises between Castle Douglas and the coast and provides a grandstand view of the Solway Firth with the Cumbrian hills beyond. The bay towards the left is the area

illustrated on pages 50/51, with Kippford just visible further up the estuary. In the centre is
Auchencairn Bay. Our route continues through the landscape on the right-hand side of this panorama.

58 Galloway is home to several great abbeys, of which Dundrennan is a further example. The first Cistercian monks arrived here in 1142; today it remains a place for peaceful contemplation.

Kirkcudbright surely ranks as one of Scotland's most attractive towns. Even at night it creates an **59** evocative scene, with the harbour in the foreground, and silhouettes of the Parish Church and castle.

60 It is a town of many colours, both natural and painted. Artistically, it is re-establishing itself as a centre for arts and crafts, following its earlier period as an artists' colony (see introduction).

Left: the Tolbooth now houses an Art Centre which provides visitors with an introduction to the story **61** of the artists' colony. Right: even the War Memorial sculpture is a particularly fine piece of work.

62 It may look formidable, but as a 16th-century construction MacLellan's Castle came too late for its primary purpose to be that of a fortress. Rather, it was conceived as a grand home for its builder,

Thomas MacLellan. This conspicuous show of wealth did not dispense with defensive capabilities altogether, but they were limited. Above: in the bowels of the castle the kitchen has been re-created.

64 Broughton House is the former home of Scottish painter E.A. Hornel, one of the Glasgow Boys. This view shows the rear elevation and the garden, which is influenced by Hornel's love of Japan.

Painstakingly preserved and recreated, it is a living museum of Hornel's life and work. This is the 65 dining room, which exemplifies the elegance of the interior of the house.

66 Heading north from Kirkcudbright brings us to the southern end of Loch Ken, with the village of Crossmichael on the opposite bank. Inset: Red Kites have been re-introduced here.

A few miles north of Loch Ken is St John's Town of Dalry. Despite its name, this is a village, one that **67** is full of picturesque corners, such as the entrance to this churchyard on an autumn day.

68 The Water of Ken rises in Galloway's northern hills and on its way to feed Loch Ken tumbles and cascades through some very photogenic locations, like this one not far from Carsphairn.

Over the fells to the east of Carsphairn, the village of Moniaive is tucked into the folds of the **69** surrounding hills. This is where the road to the Striding Arches begins (see picture on p.1).

70 Galloway Forest Park is the upland area west of the Glenkens, 373 square miles of forest, hills and lochs. On a stormy day, a patch of sunlight falls on the far side of Clatteringshaws Loch.

Starting from Clatteringshaws, Raiders Road runs for ten miles through the forest, winding along the banks of the Black Water of Dee, seen here, to Bennan by Loch Ken.

72 Galloway Forest Park offers plenty of serious hill-walking, embracing as it does some of the highest hills in southern Scotland, including several Corbetts (Scottish hills from 762m/2500ft to

914m/2999ft). This wintry panorama from Meikle Lump on the Rhinns of Kells looks north-west to the summits of Corserine and, in the distance, Shalloch on Minnoch, which is in South Ayrshire.

74 Gatehouse of Fleet lies to the south of the Galloway hills and is a gateway to them. This is the High Street, captured on a day of contrasting light, with the Clock Tower looking impressive.

Left: working water wheel at The Mill on the Fleet cotton mill which now serves as a visitor and **75** exhibition centre. Right: Cardoness Castle stands on a hill across the Fleet estuary from Gatehouse.

76 West of Gatehouse of Fleet, on high ground overlooking Wigtown Bay, are Cairn Holy Chambered Cairns, two remarkably complete Neolithic burial cairns of a type characteristic of Galloway.

Erected around 5,000 years ago, the cairn pictured on the left (Cairn Holy I) is reached first, on this occasion seen in suitably moody light. Cairn Holy II (above) is 150 metres further up the hill.

78 Returning to the Galloway Forest Park to explore its western reaches: left, wild goats look impressive. Right: in a different way, so does this waterfall in the Wood of Cree north of Newton Stewart.

It might be fair to describe Loch Trool as the jewel in the crown as far as scenery in the Galloway
Forest Park is concerned. This dawn scene rather supports that opinion.

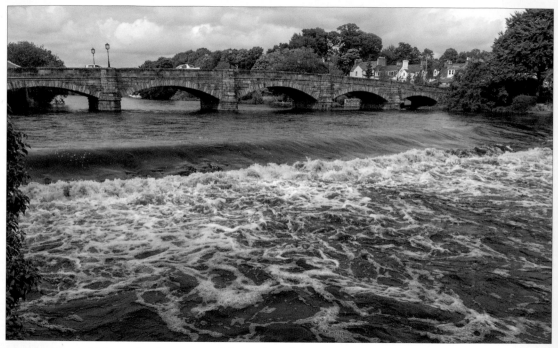

80 The river is high up the abutments of the Bridge of Cree in Newton Stewart. Being on the west bank of the Cree means this important market town is in Wigtownshire.

From Newton Stewart we delve south into the peninsula known as The Machars. Galloway is rich in **81** ancient remains: the Bronze Age Torhouse Stone Circle near Wigtown consists of 19 boulders.

82 Apart from the book festival, Wigtown deserves to be recognised in its own right as an attractive and historic market town – the older of its two mercat crosses is on the right of this picture.

The annual Wigtown Book Festival runs from late September into early October. **83**
Left and above right: two of the town's many bookshops. Lower right: the old churchyard.

84 Located in the south of The Machars, the ancient town of Whithorn grew up around the priory. The Pend is typical of the town's architecture; its shapely arch leads the way to the priory itself.

On the left is the nave of the 12th-century cathedral, the principal remnant of a far larger building. **85**
On the right stands St Ninian's Priory Parish Church, built in 1822, and still flying the flag!

86 Near Wigtown, Scotland's most southerly distillery nestles on the green banks of the River Bladnoch, from which it takes its name. It has been producing the 'Spirit of the Lowlands' since 1817.

As St Ninian brought the light of Christianity to Alba in the 390s, here we have a symbolic sunrise **87** over the Isle of Whithorn, where he established the first (known) church in Scotland.

88 Now it's time to leave The Machars behind and travel north-west into the furthest reaches of Galloway, to the tranquillity of Glenluce. What Ninian and those who followed him began

flourished throughout the land. About 800 years after Ninian, Roland, Lord of Galloway, founded
Glenluce Abbey. Much remains here – it's well worth allowing a couple of hours for your visit.

90 Glenwhan, west of Glenluce, is a garden for all seasons and full of surprises. As well as plants galore, numerous statues and sculptures add much interest. There is plenty of wildlife to see too.

A little further west again to Castle Kennedy, the picturesque remains of which stand in parkland **91** between the White Loch and the Black Loch. Here, the castle tower is seen from the walled garden.

92 Situated at the head of Loch Ryan, Stranraer is a busy ferry port with many a tale to tell. Its origins go back 500 years to the building of the Castle of St John, pictured here, around 1511.

About eight miles south-west of Stranraer, and of similar vintage, is the most attractive village and **93** harbour of Portpatrick. Inset: a black guillemot in the harbour.

94 The final leg of the journey is southwards down the Rhins of Galloway, where the mild climate allows the cultivation of exotic plants, as seen here at Logan Botanic Garden.

Left: at the southernmost tip of Scotland, in the unspoiled paradise of the Mull of Galloway, **95** stands this lighthouse. See also the back cover picture. Right: journey's end!

Published 2013 by Ness Publishing, 47 Academy Street, Elgin, Moray, IV30 1LR
Phone 01343 549663   www.nesspublishing.co.uk

All photographs © Colin Nutt except pp. 27, 48, 56/57 & 72/3 © Keith Fergus;
p.28 © www.undiscoveredscotland.co.uk; p.43 © Drumlanrig Castle; p.66 (inset) © Laurie Campbell;
p.79 © Robert Strachan; p.93 (inset) © Sue M. Cleave

Text © Colin Nutt
ISBN 978-1-906549-22-0

Front cover: sunset over Isle of Whithorn harbour; p.1: Colt Hill Striding Arch; p.4: Robert Burns statue
at Church Crescent, Dumfries; this page: Dunskey Garden; back cover: Mull of Galloway

For a list of websites and phone numbers please turn over > > > >

Websites and phone numbers (where available) for principal places featured in this book in alphabetical order:

Bladnoch Distillery: www.bladnoch.co.uk (T) 01988 402605
Broughton House: www.nts.org.uk (T) 0844 493 2246
Caerlaverock Castle: www.historic-scotland.gov.uk (T) 01387 770244
Cairn Holy Chambered Cairns: www.historic-scotland.gov.uk
Castle Kennedy: www.castlekennedygardens.co.uk (T) 01581 400225
Drumlanrig Castle: www.drumlanrig.com (T) 01848 331555
Dumfries & Galloway: www.visitdumfriesandgalloway.co.uk
Dumfries Museum and Camera Obscura: www.dumgal.gov.uk (T) 01387 253374
Dundrennan Abbey: www.historic-scotland.gov.uk (T) 01557 500262
Dunskey Garden: www.dunskey.com/walledgarden (T) 01776 810211
Ellisland Farm: www.ellislandfarm.co.uk (T) 01387 740426
Galloway Forest Park: www.gallowayforestpark.com (T) 01556 503626
Gatehouse of Fleet: www.gatehouse-of-fleet.co.uk
Glenluce Abbey: www.historic-scotland.gov.uk (T) 01581 300541
Glenwhan Gardens: www.glenwhangardens.co.uk (T) 01581 400222
Kirkcudbright: www.kirkcudbright.co.uk
Langholm: www.langholm-online.co.uk
Loch Ken: www.visitglenkens.com
Lochmaben: www.lochmaben.org.uk
Lockerbie: www.allaboutlockerbie.com
Logan Botanic Garden: www.rbge.org.uk/the-gardens/logan (T) 01776 860231
MacLellan's Castle: www.historic-scotland.gov.uk (T) 01557 331856
Moffat: www.visitmoffat.co.uk
Mull of Galloway: www.mull-of-galloway.co.uk
New (Sweetheart) Abbey: www.historic-scotland.gov.uk (T) 01387 850397
New Abbey Corn Mill: www.historic-scotland.gov.uk (T) 01387 850260